15 Instant & Irresistible

Learning Centers

That Build Early Reading & Writing Skills

Easy How-to's, Quick Tips, and Reproducible Fill-in Forms
That Invite Young Learners to Read & Write Independently

BY MARJORIE FIELDS AND DEBORAH HILLSTEAD

SCHOLASTIC
PROFESSIONAL BOOKS

New York • Toronto • London • Auckland • Sydney
Mexico City • New Delhi • Hong Kong • Buenos Aires

Dedication
For kindergarten children and teachers everywhere

Cover and interior design by **Holly Grundon**
Cover photograph by **Wanda J. Benvenutti**
Interior photographs by **Marjorie Fields and Deborah Hillstead**
Interior illustrations by **Cary Pillo**

ISBN 0-439-25182-6
Copyright © 2001 by Marjorie Fields and Deborah Hillstead
All rights reserved.
Printed in the U.S.A.

Contents

Learning Centers

Introduction

It's amazing how much writing, reading, and learning can happen in your play centers when you include literacy materials there. Just putting a note pad and pen beside the play telephone at the "house center" will generate lots of writing activity. A telephone directory by the phone will stimulate reading-like behaviors, as will a cookbook by the stove and storybooks by the doll beds.

You can extend this literacy-building concept in other pretend play themes. When your students tire of playing house, help them change the center to something else. It can become a grocery store as part of a study about foods or a hospital when the class studies health and safety. It doesn't matter what theme you use as long as you provide reasons for children to read and write.

Reading and writing during pretend play has four main advantages:

- ◎ **It helps kids think about real-world uses for reading and writing.**

- ◎ **It allows them to apply the literacy understanding accumulated from observing adult literacy behaviors.**

- ◎ **It creates a high level of motivation.**

- ◎ **It keeps them involved in the literacy activities for long periods.**

Children naturally imitate adults in pretend play. Dramatic play centers with dress-up clothes offer opportunities for role playing, commonly accepted as valuable for language development and social skills. But playing at being grown-up should involve reading and writing. When you include reading and writing materials along with other props for pretend play, you encourage literacy.

In this book, we share ideas we've used to help emergent writers explore their knowledge of reading and writing. You may have done many of these and have more ideas and themes to add. This book is intended to help you organize ideas for encouraging literacy in pretend play. Feel free to build on this foundation by adding your own ideas; then, pass it on to a fellow teacher.

We suggest 15 play themes based on experiences relevant to the kindergartners in our classes. Each theme section has six parts:

⑤ **Setting Up Your Room** describes how you can fit each pretend play theme into your classroom. The key is to find different uses for furnishings that you already have in your classroom. Children's imaginations will find possibilities you might miss.

⑤ **What's in the Prop Box?** is a list of general props for the theme. You may want to keep the props for each theme in separate boxes. Exploring these props sets the stage for learning and gets children thinking about ways to use them. Sturdy boxes with lids, such as banker's boxes (available at office-supply stores) or empty copy paper boxes, are useful for storage. (We use a suitcase to store the airport props.)

⑤ **Literacy Props** change ordinary pretend play into a literacy event. Sometimes just putting paper and pencils in a play area will encourage children to write during play.

⑤ **Questions to Encourage Literacy** will help children think of many more reasons to use writing and reading. These questions also are designed to help children understand how and why adults use reading and writing in their daily lives.

⑤ **Related Children's Books** help you integrate children's literature with the theme. We selected books that will help children think about the theme.

⑤ **Reproducible Writing Forms** are provided for your convenience. We try to use real-world writing forms, such as phone message pads, old check blanks, and recycled junk-mail materials, when possible. Field trips offer another opportunity to collect authentic literacy materials for use in your classroom. It is important that writing forms for pretend play look like those actually used by adults. Children are motivated to write by their desire to be like grown-ups.

Organization Tips

Setting the Stage

Keep props available in labeled boxes for easy access. Have prop boxes handy for when you study a related topic or when the topic comes up in children's lives. For instance, a student with a broken arm creates an interest in hospitals, or someone's plane trip leads to pretend airport play.

Discuss ways different props might be used. Help children think of reasons to write and read in each situation. Use the books listed under each play theme to help children think about the topic.

Facilitating Play

Remember: It's not play if the teacher prescribes what children should do or who plays where. Play is self-initiated and self-directed. The teacher's role is to build on children's interests and extend them.

Allow ample time for play. We recommend long periods of uninterrupted time, at least 45 minutes, to allow children's in-depth involvement. It takes quite a while for them to figure out their roles and get props arranged. Too often, playtime is over just as children are beginning to get involved. Sometimes we see classrooms where children must "rotate" to different play or work areas every few minutes. This procedure keeps children from truly engaging in any activity.

A new set of props initially may bring too many children to a play area. We just make the play area larger to accommodate the initial enthusiasm. Once the novelty wears off, you can make the play area smaller. Let a play theme continue until interest runs out; some themes will last only a few days and some can last several weeks. Adding new or different props over time extends interest.

Not all children will be interested in any one topic, but often interest is contagious. Personal experience increases interest and ability to play. We recommend teaming children who have

firsthand experience of the theme with those who do not. For example, a child who has flown on a plane can lead pretend play about air travel for those who have never flown.

Sometimes, you may have more than one pretend play center going on at a time. When you study transportation, you might have both an airport and a train station area. When we set up a grocery store, we keep the house center so there is a reason to go to the store. Use questions such as those suggested in this book to enrich and extend writing, reading, and play.

How to Get Started

When setting up a play center, think about where the children in your classroom might observe adults using reading and writing to conduct business. This might be when they go with their parents to the grocery store, the bank, the post office, or the doctor. The important thing is to help children notice how print is used in the world and to encourage them to practice what they observe. Themes we've included in this book are some we have seen children involved in, but not all may be meaningful to your students. Children must build on their own experiences and observations in pretend play. Create materials for themes relevant to your community.

Finding the Right Books

Children's books related to a theme provide the background information children need for their pretend play. When you need books about hospitals, grocery stores, construction, or whatever play theme you have, the book *A to Zoo: Subject Access to Children's Picture Books* by Carolyn and John Lima (Bowker-Greenwood, 1998) is a lifesaver! Ask a parent volunteer to help you gather books recommended for your theme.

Gathering the Props

Collecting the props can take time, but doesn't need to be expensive. After you have identified a play theme, tell parents what you need and ask them to help. Parents are your most valuable resource. Thrift stores and garage sales also are excellent inexpensive sources of supplies for your prop boxes.

Community involvement can be invaluable. Local merchants sometimes can supply commercial advertising signs or displays that your students can use for pretend play. Grocery stores have donated paper employee hats, Styrofoam trays, paper sacks, and more for our play store. Restaurants and fast-food chains have also been generous with menus, name tags with store insignia, paper cups, plates, and napkins for our play restaurant. Hospitals usually have child education programs that provide tongue depressors, bandages, and stickers. We have been able to get old X rays from children who have broken a bone. Parents who work in health care usually will offer paper gowns, face masks, and other "dress-up" props.

Of course, if money is no object, many items for prop boxes are available in school-supply catalogs.

Don't forget that children love to be involved in making things they need. For instance, they can make casts for pretend broken bones by using construction paper and tape. These have been great favorites, with everyone wanting to sign his or her name on a friend's pretend cast.

The literacy props may require some scavenging. Junk mail can supply envelopes and "stamps" sent by Reader's Digest, Easter Seals, NEA, and others. Many businesses will give you order blanks and receipt forms. Airports and plane ticket offices throw away parts of ticket forms. Ask them to toss some into a box for you. Collect clipboards of all kinds—they make any paper seem "official."

Ready? Let's go!

Play House

The pretend house is the play center most commonly found in kindergarten classrooms. The roles of parents are generally claimed first, but remind students that the roles of children and even pets are important. We often extend the play house center to include other center themes, such as the grocery store (page 13). Sometimes we even have a home office so "working parents" won't need day care.

Setting Up Your Room

Most kindergartens have a pretend play center with child-sized furniture that includes a table and chairs, stove, sink and refrigerator, doll beds, high chairs, and shopping carts or strollers, as well as some sort of storage system for organizing dress-up clothes and doll clothes. Children need teacher help to keep the center tidy, organized, and attractive so it nurtures quality play.

What's in the Prop Box?

- Dress-up clothes for mothers, fathers, and babies
- Baby dolls of various ethnicity
- Clothes, diapers, and blankets for dolls
- Play dishes and cooking utensils
- Pretend food
- Broom and dustpan
- Tablecloth

- What else?

_____

_____

_____

_____

Literacy Props

- Shopping list (page 11)
- To Do list (page 11)
- Checks (page 12)
- Phone message pad (page 12)
- Phone book and telephone
- Cookbooks, blank recipe cards, and file box
- Bedtime storybooks
- Newspapers
- Writing paper
- Envelopes and stamps
- Pens and pencils
- **Work sheets** (Children in the play family can do their homework after dinner.)
- What else? _____

Questions to Encourage Literacy

- How can we find someone's phone number?
- Why do we write down phone messages?
- How do we learn how to cook something?
- Where can you write favorite recipes?
- Why is it important to make a list before you go to the store?
- How can we remember our appointments?
- Why do we make a "to do" list?
- Would Grandma want a letter about what your baby can do?

Related Children's Books

Bigmama's
by Donald Crews
(Mulberry, 1998)

Julius, the Baby of the World
by Kevin Henkes
(Mulberry, 1995)

Mama, Do You Love Me?
by Barbara M. Joosse
(Chronicle, 1998)

Just Me and My Dad
by Mercer Meyer
(Western Publishing, 1978)

Five Minutes' Peace
by Jill Murphy
(Penguin Putnam, 1999)

On Mother's Lap
by Ann Herbert Scott
(Houghton Mifflin, 1992)

We Were Tired of Living in a House
by Liesel Moak Skorpen
(Penguin Putnam, 1999)

We need a list
when we shop,
to know what to buy
and when to stop!

1. _____

2. _____

3. _____

4. _____

5. _____

6. _____

7. _____

8. _____

9. _____

10. _____

11. _____

12. _____

13. _____

14. _____

Things To Do Today!

1. _____

2. _____

3. _____

4. _____

5. _____

6. _____

7. _____

8. _____

First Independent
Bank of Kindergarten

Date _____

Pay to the order of: _____

In the amount of: _____ $ _____

Memo: _____

Signature _____

Phone Message

For _____

Date _____ **Time** _____

Name _____

Phone _____ **Ext.** _____

○ Telephoned   ○ Please call back
○ Called to see you   ○ Will call again
○ Returned your call ○ Important

Message _____
_____
_____
_____

Phone Message

For _____

Date _____ **Time** _____

Name _____

Phone _____ **Ext.** _____

○ Telephoned   ○ Please call back
○ Called to see you   ○ Will call again
○ Returned your call ○ Important

Message _____
_____
_____
_____

Grocery Store

As part of our nutrition unit, we take children on a field trip to the grocery store to buy ingredients for "stone soup." Creating balanced-menu grocery lists and playing grocery store back in the classroom offer children a rich opportunity to practice their literacy skills.

Setting Up Your Room

Place the grocery store center next to the play house center so children in the play house can go shopping in the store. To set up the grocery store, all you need is a table for the check-out counter and empty shelving on which to stack different foods.

What's in the Prop Box?

- Aprons for the storekeepers
- Hats for storekeepers
- Cash register
- Play money
  (can be made by children)
- Calculators
- Shopping cart
- Clean, empty food containers
  (no glass)

- Styrofoam trays for pretend food
- What else?

  _____

  _____

  _____

  _____

  _____

Literacy Props

- Shopping list (page 11)
- Order forms to restock store (page 15)
- Price tags (page 15)
- On Sale sign (page 16)
- Grocery ads, coupons
- Adding-machine paper rolls for receipts
- Pencils, pens, markers
- What else? _____

Questions to Encourage Literacy

- Why do storekeepers need to write?
- How can people find out what is on sale each day?
- How do shoppers know how much things cost?
- How can you help yourself remember what to buy at the store?
- What is a receipt and why do you need one?
- How can the storekeeper keep track of what groceries to order?

Add Your Ideas:

_____

_____

Related Children's Books

Do the Doors Open by Magic? and Other Supermarket Questions
by Catherine Riply
(Firefly Books, 1995)

On Market Street
by Arnold Lobel
(William Morrow, 1989)

Stone Soup
by Marcia Brown
(Aladdin, 1987)

Tommy at the Grocery Store
by Bill Grossman
(HarperCollins, 1991)

Thank you for
shopping at our store.
We hope you found
what you're looking for.

If you did not
we'd like to know.
Please write it down
before you go.

1. _____

2. _____

3. _____

4. _____

5. _____

6. _____

7. _____

8. _____

9. _____

10. _____

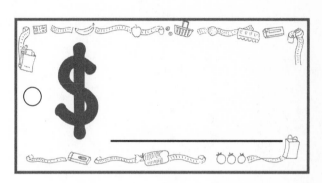

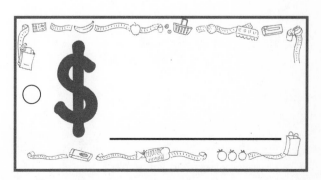

On SALE this week!

for only $ _____ : ____

for only $ _____ : ____

for only $ _____ : ____

for only $ _____ : ____

Restaurant

A restaurant is a natural theme to follow the grocery store. Baking and other class cooking projects contribute to restaurant play as children reenact their cooking experiences. "Customers" reading menus and "waiters" taking orders both encourage literacy.

Setting Up Your Room

You can easily convert your play house center into a restaurant. Chefs can cook in the kitchen and customers can sit at the table and chairs.

What's in the Prop Box?

- Hats and aprons for waiters and waitresses
- Plates, cups, bowls, and silverware
- Cash register
- Calculators
- Pretend money
- Play dough for pretend food
- Containers and wrappers from fast-food chains
- What else?

_____

_____

_____

Literacy Props

- 🌀 Menus (page 19)
- 🌀 Order pad/bill (page 20)
- 🌀 Menus from actual restaurants
- 🌀 Name tags for waiters and waitresses
- 🌀 Dry-erase boards for writing daily specials
- 🌀 Pens, pencils, markers
- 🌀 What else? _____

_____

Questions to Encourage Literacy

- 🌀 How do waiters remember what you ordered?
- 🌀 How do they remember where you sit?
- 🌀 How does the cook know what to fix?
- 🌀 How do the customers know about the "special of the day" or the "burger of the month"?

Add Your Ideas:

_____

_____

_____

_____

Related Children's Books

Babar Learns to Cook
by Laurent de Brunhoff
(Random House, 1978)

D.W. the Picky Eater
by Marc Brown
(Little Brown, 1997)

Eating Out
by Helen Oxenbury
(Dial Books, 1983)

Little Nino's Pizzeria
by Karen Barbour
(Harcourt Brace, 1990)

The Berenstain Bears Cook-It!
by Stan Berenstain
(Random House, 1996)

salad $2.00

pizza $3.00

french fries $1.00

hamburger $1.00

hot dog $1.00

_____ . . $ _____

_____ . . $ _____

_____ . . $ _____

_____ . . $ _____

_____ . . $ _____

(fold here next)

(fold here first)

Thanks for Coming!

Please let us know
how we're doing!

_____ **Great!**

_____ **Good**

_____ **Fair**

_____ **Try Harder!**

_____

_____

_____

COOKS CHOICE RESTAURANT
Menu

Eat Now!

Total	

Thank you for dining with us!

Eat Now!

Total	

Thank you for dining with us!

Eat Now!

Total	

Thank you for dining with us!

Eat Now!

Total	

Thank you for dining with us!

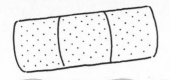
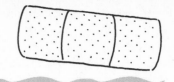

Hospital

We study doctors and hospitals as part of our "Community Helpers" social studies unit. We take children on a field trip to the hospital where they learn not to be afraid of doctors and nurses. During the field trip, we point out to children ways medical personnel use reading and writing, as well as explain the importance of the charts and records.

Setting Up Your Room

Drape a sheet on a classroom table to simulate a hospital bed. Use an empty shelving unit to store medical supplies. Arrange children's chairs to create a waiting room.

What's in the Prop Box?

- White flat sheets
- Jackets for nurses and doctors
- Nurses' caps, face masks, plastic gloves
- Stethoscopes (real or toy)
- Disposable thermometers
- Tongue depressors
- Small containers for pretend medicine
- Bandages, tape, rolls of gauze
- What else?

Literacy Props

- Patient information form (page 23)
- Prescription pad (page 23)
- Check-in form (page 24)
- Appointment cards (page 24)
- Insurance forms
- Clipboards with paper and pencil attached
- Name tags, paper strips for I.D. wrist bands
- Books and magazines for the waiting room
- Folders for medical records
- Pens, pencils, markers
- What else? _____

Questions to Encourage Literacy

- What do doctors and nurses need to write?
- How does the doctor know about your health problems?
- Who fills out the insurance forms?
- How do you pay the doctor?
- Doctor, does the patient need a prescription for some medicine?
- Patient, do you want your friends to sign your cast?

Add Your Ideas:

_____

_____

Related Children's Books

Curious George Goes to the Hospital
by Margret and H.A. Rey
(Houghton Mifflin, 1966)

Corduroy Goes to the Doctor
by Don Freeman
(Viking, 1987)

The Skeleton Inside You
by Philip Balestrino
(HarperTrophy, 1989)

The Magic School Bus Inside the Human Body
by Joanna Cole
(Scholastic, 1993)

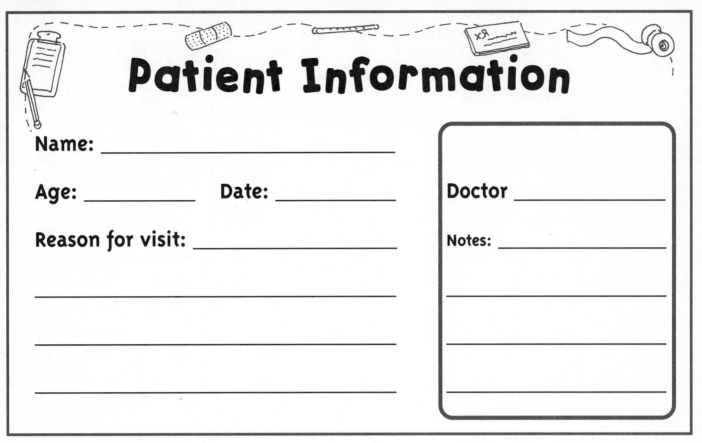

Patient Information

Name: _____

Age: _____   Date: _____

Reason for visit: _____

_____

_____

_____

Doctor _____

Notes: _____

_____

_____

_____

Prescription

Name: _____

Age: _____

Date: _____

_____
Doctor's Signature

Prescription

Name: _____

Age: _____

Date: _____

_____
Doctor's Signature

Come and sit down
if you're sick.
Write your name here
really quick.

The Doctor is **IN**

Have a seat
in this room
and the Doctor
will see you soon.

1. _____

2. _____

3. _____

4. _____

5. _____

6. _____

7. _____

8. _____

9. _____

10. _____

11. _____

12. _____

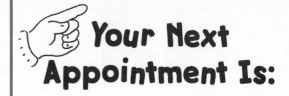

Your Next Appointment Is:

Day: _____

Time: _____

Your Next Appointment Is:

Day: _____

Time: _____

Your Next Appointment Is:

Day: _____

Time: _____

Post Office

Studying the post office is also part of our "Community Helpers" unit. We usually do this theme in February for writing and mailing valentines. A field trip to the post office will give children a behind-the-scenes view of how postal-service employees use literacy. All these experiences and observations become part of post office play back in the classroom.

Setting Up Your Room

To turn the play house center into a post office, turn around the stove to make a counter and put the table beside it for processing mail. Convert the cupboards into post-office boxes by adding small, lidless boxes turned on their sides.

What's in the Prop Box?

- Mail carrier hats and bags
- Postal worker uniform shirt
- Rubber stamps and stamp pads
- Small scale for postage
- Cash register
- Play money
- Class mailbox
- What else?

_____

Literacy Props

- Envelopes (page 27)
- Pretend stamps (page 27)
- Stationery (page 28)
- Junk mail forms to fill out
- Junk mail return envelopes
- Return address labels
- Address book
- Materials to label individual mailboxes
- Pens, pencils, markers
- What else? _____

Questions to Encourage Literacy

- Who are you going to write to?
- What are you going to write about?
- How will the person know who wrote the letter?
- How will he or she know where to send back a letter?
- How does the mail carrier know where to deliver your letter?

Add Your Ideas:

_____

_____

Related Children's Books

A Letter to Amy
by Ezra Jack Keats
(Penguin Putnam, 1998)

Mail Carriers
by Dee Ready
(Bridgestone, 1998)

Mailing May
by Michael O. Tunnel
(HarperCollins, 2000)

The Jolly Postman or Other People's Letters
by Janet and Allan Ahlberg
(Little Brown, 1986)

The Post Office Book: Mail and How It Moves
by Gail Gibbons
(HarperTrophy, 1986)

Messages in the Mailbox: How to Write a Letter
by Loreen Leedy
(Holiday House, 1994)

Note Cards for Post Office

Write the address on the front and the message on the back. Fold on lines and secure with glue stick or tape.

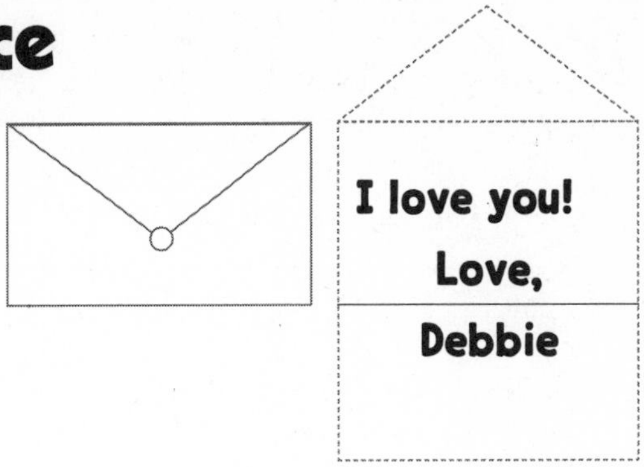

I love you!
Love,
Debbie

Stamps for Post Office

Cut along the dashed lines

fold line

From:

To: _____

_____

_____

fold line

School

Children naturally imitate their teachers and play school. This theme can continue throughout the year. Fortunately, the props are always available—any pointers, books, paper, and pencils turn into teacher props when children sit in the teacher's chair. Literacy, of course, is a natural part of playing school.

Setting Up Your Room

The whole room is an appropriate setting, but usually the gathering area in front of the teacher's chair is viewed as the prime spot.

What's in the Prop Box?

(They're **ALL** literacy props!)

- Attendance/roll call form (page 31)
- Lesson plan book (page 31)
- Old attendance/record books
- Lap chalkboards or white boards
- Colored chalk
- Paper in different sizes, shapes, and colors
- Old writing journals
- Old workbooks and ditto sheets
- What else?

Borrow from the Teacher's Supplies

- Familiar storybooks
- Flannel board and figures
- Pocket chart and insert cards
- Magnet letters
- Big books and pointers
- Teacher's chair
- What else? _____

Questions to Encourage Literacy

- What kinds of things do teachers need to write down?
- How do they remember who has learned what?
- How do they let parents know when there is meeting?
- What are you going to read for story time today, Teacher?
- Are you going to let your students tell a story on the flannel board?
- What kind of writing are your students going to do today?

Add Your Ideas:

_____

_____

Related Children's Books

Bea and Mr. Jones
by Amy Schwarts
(Simon & Schuster, 1994)

Curious George Goes to School
by Margret and H.A. Rey
(Houghton Mifflin, 1989)

Miss Nelson Is Missing!
by Harry Allard
(Houghton Mifflin, 1985)

My Great-Aunt Arizona
by Gloria Houston
(HarperCollins, 1992)

Teachers Help Us Learn
by Carol Greene
(Child's World, 1997)

The Berenstain Bears' Trouble at School
by Stan and Jan Berenstain
(Random House, 1987)

Will I Have a Friend?
by Miriam Cohen
(Aladdin, 1989)

Lesson Plans for _____

Teacher: _____

1st

2nd

3rd

Children, children, please come near so we can find out who is here!

Here (x)

Names:

Zoo Office

For this theme, any office will work—one that children actually can visit, such as a parent's office, is best. We use the zoo office because the children have a chance to visit there during a field trip to the zoo. Whatever kind of office you visit, make sure to gather literacy props appropriate to that office. The visit and the props will stimulate office play.

Setting Up Your Room

Add telephones, "in" and "out" baskets, and other office supplies to turn classroom tables into office desks.

What's in the Prop Box?

- Zoo posters
- Zoo animal figures
- Telephone
- What else?

_____

_____

_____

_____

Literacy Props

- Order forms (page 34)
- Zoo tickets (page 34)
- Weekly schedule (page 35)
- Envelopes and stamps (page 36)
- Phone message pads (page 12)
- "In" and "out" baskets
- Paper clips, rubber bands, staplers
- Stamps and stamp pads
- Name tags for office workers
- Books about zoo animal care
- Pens, pencils, markers
- What else? _____

Questions to Encourage Literacy

- Why does the zoo need an office?
- What do workers do there?
- How do they know when to order food for the animals?
- How do they schedule school visits so everyone doesn't come at once?
- Why do people call the zoo office?
- Do they need to take messages?

Add Your Ideas:

_____

_____

Related Children's Books

A Children's Zoo
by Tana Hoban
(Greenwillow, 1985)

At the Zoo
by Heather Amery
(EDC Publications, 1994)

Curious George Visits the Zoo
by Margret and H.A. Rey
(Houghton Mifflin, 1985)

If I Ran the Zoo
by Dr. Seuss
(Random House, 1989)

Zoo
by Gail Gibbons
(Crowell, 1987)

Please order for the ...

Zoo Ticket

$ _____

good for _____

Zoo Ticket

$ _____

good for _____

Please order for the ...

Zoo Ticket

$ _____

good for _____

Zoo Ticket

$ _____

good for _____

Weekly Schedule

	Monday	Tuesday	Wednesday	Thursday	Friday	Saturday	Sunday
9:00							
10:00							
11:00							
12:00							
1:00							
2:00							
3:00							
4:00							
5:00							
6:00							

Zoo Visit Confirmation Cards

Write the address on the front and the message on the back. Fold on lines and secure with glue stick or tape.

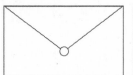

Your zoo trip will be on ...

Thank you, Zookeeper

Cut along the dashed lines

Stamps for Cards

fold line

Zoo Office Room # _____

To: _____

_____

_____

fold line

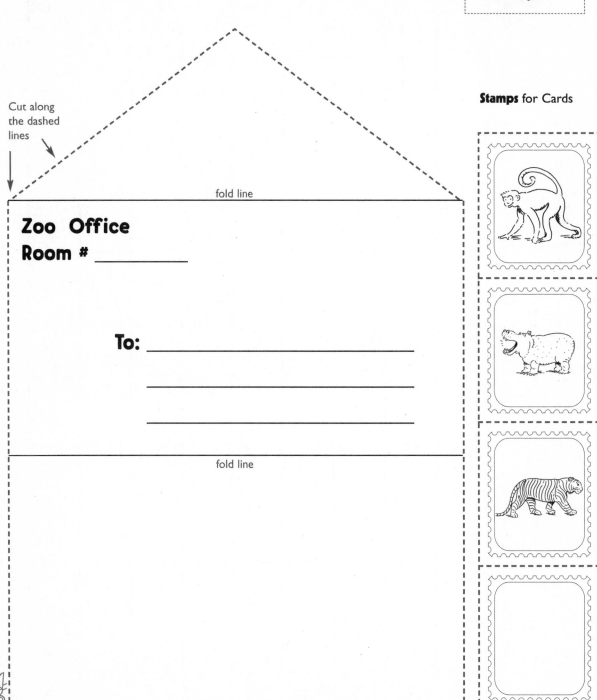

Pet Store

We combine a study of pets with a focus on responsibility—a major life skill that can be learned by caring for a pet—and the pet store. Children research their pet of choice and find out how to care for it before going to a nearby pet store and pretending to buy it. After a visit, they naturally want to play pet store. We make sure to include literacy props for them.

Setting Up Your Room

Clear a set of shelves for displaying stuffed animals and pet supplies, such as food bowls, cages, and fish bowls. A small table can become the store counter where children make their purchases.

What's in the Prop Box?

- ⑤ Pet tags
- ⑤ Collars and leashes
- ⑤ Pet combs and brushes
- ⑤ Stuffed animals
- ⑤ Pet beds
- ⑤ Cages
- ⑤ Fish bowls
- ⑤ Pet food boxes and bowls
- ⑤ What else?

_____

_____

_____

Literacy Props

- Price list (page 39)
- Receipts (page 40)
- Price tags (page 15)
- Adding machine and roll of paper
- Pet data folders
- Pet licenses
- Note pads
- Telephone and phone book
- Play money
- Pens and pencils
- What else? _____

Questions to Encourage Literacy

- How will you know how to take care of your pet?
- How can you tell what kind of pet is best for you?
- How do you know how much the pets cost?
- How do pet stores get pets?
- What do you do to get a pet license?

Add Your Ideas:

_____

_____

Related Children's Books

Good Dog, Carl
by Alexandra Day
(Aladdin, 1997)

Franklin Wants a Pet
by Paulette Bourgeois
(Scholastic, 1995)

Have You Seen My Cat?
by Eric Carle
(Aladdin, 1997)

How Kittens Grow
by Millicent E. Selsam
(Scholastic, 1992)

Millions of Cats
by Wanda Gag
(Paper Star, 1996)

My Puppy Is Born
by Joanna Cole
(Mulberry, 1989)

Pet Show!
by Ezra Jack Keats
(Aladdin, 1987)

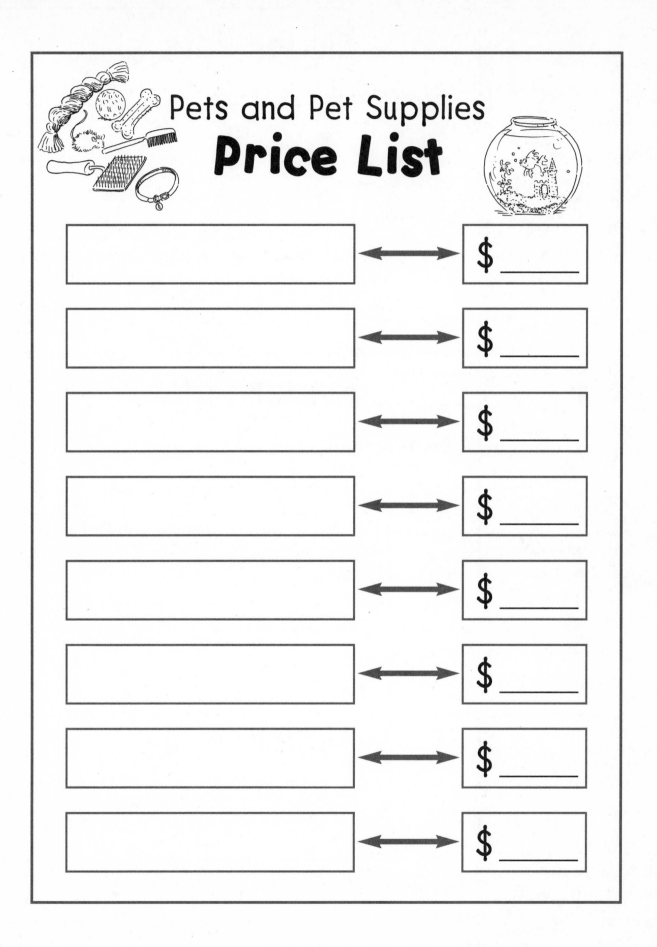

Pets and Pet Supplies
Price List

$ _____

$ _____

$ _____

$ _____

$ _____

$ _____

$ _____

$ _____

Kinder-Pets

received from _____

the sum of _____

for _____ on _____

Come on in and buy a pet! What kind would you like to get?

Kinder-Pets

received from _____

the sum of _____

for _____ on _____

Come on in and buy a pet! What kind would you like to get?

Kinder-Pets

received from _____

the sum of _____

for _____ on _____

Come on in and buy a pet! What kind would you like to get?

Shoe Store

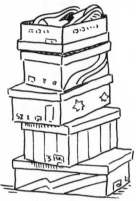

This theme came about as we were doing a math activity comparing shoes. Children visit shoe stores with their parents, making this a familiar theme. Opportunities for matching and measuring add math to this play. Literacy is involved in labeling shoes, keeping inventory, and writing orders.

Setting Up Your Room

Line up children's chairs for customers to sit on while trying on shoes. The cash register can turn a classroom table into the sales desk. Clear shelving for shoe display.

What's in the Prop Box?

- Assorted shoes and boots
- Shoe brush
- Shoe boxes
- Tissue paper
- Shoe horns
- "Footsies," knee-hi nylons, socks
- Foot measure (a ruler works great!)
- Shoelaces
- Polishing sponges (free for guests in hotel rooms)
- Cash register
- Play money
- What else?

_____

_____

_____

_____

Literacy Props

- ⟲ Receipts (page 43)
- ⟲ Order forms (page 43)
- ⟲ Checks (page 12)
- ⟲ On Sale sign (page 16)
- ⟲ Shoe advertisements
- ⟲ Shoe pictures, catalogs, and posters
- ⟲ Turn tickets
- ⟲ Clipboard with paper attached
- ⟲ Pens or pencils
- ⟲ What else? _____

Questions to Encourage Literacy

- ⟲ How do you know what size shoes you wear?
- ⟲ What kind of shoes do you need?
- ⟲ How can you tell if the shoes fit?
- ⟲ How much do they cost?
- ⟲ How will you pay for them?
- ⟲ How do you know what is on sale?
- ⟲ How do you know who gets a "good customer" discount?
- ⟲ How does the store keep track of how many shoes are sold?

Add Your Ideas:

_____

Related Children's Books

Big Sarah's Little Boots
by Paulette Bourgeois
(Econo-Clad, 1999)

Shoes from Grandpa
by Mem Fox
(Orchard Books, 1992)

Shoe Town
by Janet Stevens and
Susan Stevens Crummel
(Green Light Readers, 1999)

The Growing-Up Feet
by Beverly Cleary
(William Morrow, 1987)

The Elves and the Shoemaker
by the Brothers Grimm
(Barefoot Books, 1998)

We have shoes, in sets of two. Come on in and see what's new!

School Shoe Stores of America

received from _____

the sum of _____

for _____ pairs of shoes, on _____

We have shoes, in sets of two. Come on in and see what's new!

School Shoe Stores of America

received from _____

the sum of _____

for _____ pairs of shoes, on _____

Please Order the Following Shoes

How Many	Size	Color	Type of shoe

 # Hair Salon

Children learn to appreciate ethnic diversity when they're exposed to different hair types. Pretending to visit a hair salon encourages practice in appropriate public behaviors, such as waiting patiently and conversing quietly. Books and magazines in the waiting room encourage literacy.

IMPORTANT:

Be careful not to put scissors in the hair salon; haircuts are not part of the services in a kindergarten center. Also, be sure to screen for head lice before starting this theme.

Setting Up Your Room

Recycle your play house furniture for the hair salon. Stylists can pretend to wash customers' hair in the pretend sink. Drape a cloth over the stove and prop a mirror against the stove's back for a hair-dressing "station." Set up chairs for clients to sit on.

What's in the Prop Box?

- ⑥ Hair clips and other accessories
- ⑥ Combs
- ⑥ Curlers
- ⑥ Mirrors
- ⑥ Hair dryer
- ⑥ Aprons, rubber gloves
- ⑥ Spray and shampoo bottles
- ⑥ Towels, shower caps
- ⑥ What else?

_____

Literacy Props

- List of services (page 46)
- Sign-in sheet (page 46)
- Checks (page 12)
- Phone message pads (page 12)
- Appointment cards (page 24)
- Weekly schedule (page 35)
- Phone and phone book
- Magazines, book of hairstyles
- Clipboards
- "Credit cards"
- Computer
- Pencils and pens
- What else? _____

Questions to Encourage Literacy

- How do you decide on a hairstyle?
- How will you remember the time of your appointment?
- How will the hair stylist remember when is your appointment?
- Why are there magazines at the salon?

Add Your Ideas:

_____

_____

Related Children's Books

Amanda's Perfect Hair
by Linda Milstein
(William Morrow, 1993)

Bad Hair Day
by Susan Hood
(Grosset & Dunlap, 1999)

*Junie B. Jones
Is a Beauty Shop Guy*
by Barbara Park
(Random House, 1998)

Mop Top
by Don Freeman
(Viking Press, 1978)

I want my hair:

☐ curly . . . .

☐ straight . . . .

☐ ponytail . . . .

☐ pigtails . . . .

☐ braided . . . .

☐ other ideas? . . .

I want my hair:

☐ curly . . . .

☐ straight . . . .

☐ ponytail . . . .

☐ pigtails . . . .

☐ braided . . . .

☐ other ideas? . . .

Please sign in.

1. _____

2. _____

3. _____

4. _____

5. _____

6. _____

Please sign in.

1. _____

2. _____

3. _____

4. _____

5. _____

6. _____

Library

In this center, children replicate school library procedures in their own classroom library. They write their names on library cards and read the date stamps to find out when books are due. You can leave this center open all year-round.

Setting Up Your Room

Your classroom library area is a perfect spot for this play theme. Books in the class library can be "checked out" and returned there. Set up a computer on a classroom table to serve as the Check In/Out desk. You may want to expand the library to include your listening center for books with tapes.

What's in the Prop Box?

- ⑥ Book order catalogs
- ⑥ Newspapers
- ⑥ Library cards
- ⑥ Bar-code stickers
- ⑥ Book pockets for due date cards
- ⑥ Telephone
- ⑥ What else?

_____

_____

Literacy Props

- ⊚ Overdue notices (page 49)
- ⊚ Due date cards (page 49)
- ⊚ Check-out and overdue lists (page 50)
- ⊚ Date stamp and stamp pad
- ⊚ Publishers catalog
- ⊚ Books, audio book sets, and magazines
- ⊚ Labels and signs
- ⊚ Paper
- ⊚ Pencils and markers
- ⊚ What else? _____

Questions to Encourage Literacy

- ⊚ How do you get a library card?
- ⊚ How do you borrow things from the library?
- ⊚ How do you find a special book?
- ⊚ How does the library know who has a book?
- ⊚ How do you know when a book must be back?
- ⊚ How do books get back in their places?

Add Your Ideas:

_____

_____

_____

Related Children's Books

Check it Out! The Book About Libraries
by Gail Gibbons
(Harcourt Brace, 1988)

I Took My Frog to the Library
by Eric A. Kimmel
(Puffin, 1992)

Librarians
by Dee Ready
(Bridgestone Books, 1998)

The Librarian from the Black Lagoon
by Mike Thaler
(Scholastic, 1997)

The Library Dragon
by Carmen Agra Deedy
(Peachtree, 1994)

Name: _____

Hurry! Hurry!
We can't wait.
Return your book.
It's late, late, late!

Book Title: _____

_____

_____

Date Due: _____

Name: _____

Hurry! Hurry!
We can't wait.
Return your book.
It's late, late, late!

Book Title: _____

_____

_____

Date Due: _____

Classroom Library

Book Title: _____

_____
Due Date

_____
Due Date

_____
Due Date

_____
Due Date

Classroom Library

Book Title: _____

_____
Due Date

_____
Due Date

_____
Due Date

_____
Due Date

Books Checked Out

Overdue Books

Airport

We like to begin this study with a trip to the airport. We have been fortunate to see behind the scenes where luggage is transferred and food service is loaded. Ticket agents willingly explain the importance of literacy at the airport: to make sure luggage gets to the right place, to help passengers get on the right plane, and to ensure that the pilot knows where to go. We collect forms at the airport for use in the play center back in the classroom.

Setting Up Your Room

Place a classroom computer on a desk for check in. Arrange chairs to simulate plane seating and use media carts for meal and beverage carts. Children also may want to set up a luggage-claim area.

What's in the Prop Box?

(Use a suitcase for this prop box to help set the tone.)

- Cloth bags for carry-on bags
- Airplane pillows
- Seat belts
- Earphones for movies and music
- Trays for flight attendants
- What else?

_____

_____

Literacy Props

- Ticket/boarding pass (page 53)
- Passenger list (page 53)
- Luggage-identification tags (page 54)
- Personal identification card (page 54)
- Order pads for flight attendants (page 20)
- Plane schedules, travel brochures
- Magazines for on the plane
- Safety instruction cards
- What else? _____

Questions to Encourage Literacy

- Where can you find ideas for vacations?
- How do you know what time to be at the airport?
- How do you get a ticket to go on a plane?
- What information needs to be on the ticket?
- How do luggage handlers know on what plane to put your suitcase?
- How do you know which suitcase is yours?
- How do flight attendants know what you want to eat and drink?
- How do you know how to be safe on the plane?

Add Your Ideas:

_____

Related Children's Books

Airplanes and Flying Machines
by Pascale De Bourgoing
(Scholastic, 1992)

Airport
by Byron Barton
(HarperTrophy, 1987)

Fly Away Home
by Eve Bunting
(Clarion, 1993)

Flying
by Donald Crews
(Mulberry, 1989)

The Berenstain Bears Fly-It!
by Stan and Jan Berenstain
(Random House, 1996)

Up in the Air
by Myra Cohn Livingston
(Holiday House, 1989)

Kinder-Airline Boarding Pass

Name: _____

Destination: _____

Departure: _____

Arrival: _____

Kinder-Airline Boarding Pass

Name: _____

Destination: _____

Departure: _____

Arrival: _____

Kinder-Airline Boarding Pass

Name: _____

Destination: _____

Departure: _____

Arrival: _____

Airline Passenger List

For: _____
(today's date)

_____

_____

_____

_____

_____

_____

_____
Name

_____
Room#

(picture)

This is my bag!

◯

_____

This is my bag!

◯

_____
Name

_____
Room#

(picture)

This is my bag!

◯

_____

This is my bag!

◯

_____
Name

_____
Room#

(picture)

This is my bag!

◯

_____

Engineering & Construction

We like to take students to see construction sites near school. This stimulates pretend construction in the block center. Children draw plans for their buildings on graph paper and make lists of materials they need. They also create and post signs about their building plans, modeled after the signs they have observed at actual sites.

Setting Up Your Room

The best place for this play theme is usually the block center. Building materials are crucial to getting into the role. Other kinds of materials children can use besides blocks include tape, clay, glue, paper, straws, and crayons.

What's in the Prop Box?

- ⑥ Measuring tapes
- ⑥ Hard hats
- ⑥ Tools and tool belts
- ⑥ Surveyor's tapes (found at hardware stores)
- ⑥ Protective goggles
- ⑥ Work gloves
- ⑥ Boots
- ⑥ First-aid kit
- ⑥ Briefcase
- ⑥ Walkie-talkies
- ⑥ Lunch boxes

- ⑥ What else?

_____

_____

_____

_____

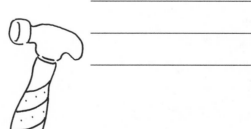

Literacy Props

- Planning grid or graph paper (page 57)
- Caution and construction signs
- Time cards
- Telephone and phone book
- Business cards
- Blueprints, maps
- Design magazine
- Clipboards with paper attached
- Rulers, pencils, and pens
- What else? _____

Questions to Encourage Literacy

- How do construction workers know what to build?
- How do they know how to build it?
- How do architects and engineers share their plans?
- How do workers know what supplies they have and what they need?
- How do workers get more building materials if they run out?
- How do workers get paid?

Add Your Ideas:

_____

_____

Related Children's Books

Mike Mulligan and his Steam Shovel
by Virginia Lee Burton
(Houghton Mifflin, 1977)

Building a House
by Byron Barton
(William Morrow, 1981)

Construction Zone
by Tana Hoban
(Greenwillow, 1997)

Machines at Work
by Byron Barton
(HarperCollins, 1997)

Jobs People Do: A Day in the Life of a Builder
by Linda Hayward
(Dorling Kindersley, 2001)

Commercial Fishing

While this theme is a natural success in areas where children are familiar with the industry, it can also spark the imagination of children living in landlocked areas. If possible, invite a fisherman to discuss literacy materials, such as tide books, marine charts, and fishing licenses. You may also want to show a video about commercial fishing.

Setting Up Your Room

Encourage children to make a pretend boat using chairs, tables, large cardboard boxes, and butcher paper.

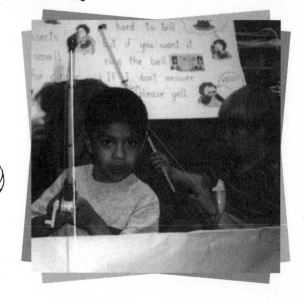

What's in the Prop Box?

- Life jackets, life buoy
- Rain gear, boots
- Pretend fish
- Boat wheel, anchor
- Binoculars
- Radio
- Floats, nets, poles
- Scales
- Lights
- Compass
- "Fish finder" (depth indicator)
- Cooler, Styrofoam for pretend dry ice

- What else?

_____

_____

_____

Literacy Props

- ⑥ Fishing log book (page 60)
- ⑥ Fishing license (page 60)
- ⑥ Marine charts and maps
- ⑥ Tide book
- ⑥ Boat diary
- ⑥ Weather reports
- ⑥ Fish I.D. poster, fishing magazines
- ⑥ Fish tickets and receipts
- ⑥ Fish cookbooks
- ⑥ Tape measure
- ⑥ What else? _____

Questions to Encourage Literacy

- ⑥ How do you know where to fish?
- ⑥ How do you find your way to fishing spots?
- ⑥ How do you steer your boat safely?
- ⑥ How do you know when the weather is safe for the boat?
- ⑥ How do you get money for your fish?
- ⑥ How do you keep track of how many fish you have caught and how many you have sold?

Add Your Ideas:

_____

_____

Related Children's Books

Big Al
by Andrew Clements
(Aladdin, 1997)

Blue Sea
by Robert Kalan
(Mulberry, 1992)

Island Boy
by Barbara Cooney
(Viking, 1989)

The Rainbow Fish
by Marcus Pfister
(North South Books, 1992)

Gone Fishing
by Earlene Long
(Houghton Mifflin, 1987)

Who Sank the Boat?
by Pamela Allan
(Paper Star, 1996)

**Fisherman, Fisherman!
Can you say
what kinds of fish
did you catch today?**

1. _____

2. _____

3. _____

4. _____

5. _____

6. _____

**You can count the fish
that are here to stay!**

_____

**But can you count the
ones that got away?**

_____

_____

**The Kindergarten
Department of Fisheries**

Awards this license to:

_____

for the year of _____

**The Kindergarten
Department of Fisheries**

Awards this license to:

_____

for the year of _____

Native American Fish Camp

(Written in consultation with Helen Abbott Watkins, keeper of the culture for her Tlingit heritage)

Introduce children to this traditional subsistence food-gathering event that has enormous cultural significance for Native Americans in Alaska and the Pacific Northwest. Many urban and rural native families travel to their traditional family fishing sites for a few weeks each summer to catch, fillet, and dry their own salmon. They also gather and preserve berries and seaweeds.

Setting Up Your Room

You may want to put away your play house or block area to make room for a tent and other props for the duration of the fish camp.

What's in the Prop Box?

- Tent-making props, camp stove

- Smokehouse props: salmon drying sticks, pretend salmon strips, pretend smokehouse fire (try stones and wood with flashlight under red crepe paper)

- Rope, fishing poles, and nets

- Life vests, buoys, boat motor, and anchor

- Rubber boots, mosquito head nets

- Pretend fish, plastic tubs for fish

- Fish club, fish-cleaning gloves

- Toy wheelbarrow to transport fish

- Enamel pot for canning salmon

- Canning containers

- Berries and berry buckets

- Real or pretend dried seaweed

- Water jugs

- Cardboard for making pretend boats

Literacy Props

- Fishing diary (pages 63-64)
- Fishing license (page 60)
- Grocery list (page 11)
- Fish smoking and canning recipes
- Contact numbers for pager, cell phone, CB or VHF radios
- Boating safety information
- Marine maps, tide books
- Magazines
- Timers
- Measuring tools
- Paper and pencils
- What else? _____

Questions to Encourage Literacy

- How do you get a permit to fish?
- How do you know how many fish of each kind you are allowed to catch?
- How can you remember how many fish you caught?
- How do you know when water and weather conditions are right for fishing?
- How do you know where to go for fish?

Add Your Ideas:

_____

Related Children's Books

A Salmon for Simon
by Betty Waterton
(Groundwood Books, 1998)

A River Dream
by Allen Say
(Houghton Mifflin, 1993)

Blueberries for Sal
by Robert McCloskey
(Viking Press, 1987)

Fish Eyes
by Lois Ehlert
(Harcourt Brace, 1992)

Kahtahah
by Frances Lackey Paul
(Alaska Northwest, 1996)

Swimmy
by Leo Lionni
(Knopf, 1991)

The Girl Who Swam With the Fish: An Athabascan Legend
by Michelle Renner
(Alaska Northwest, 1995)

Just for fun, I ___

Today I ___

I like to _____

When it rains _____